WOMEN IN SCIENCE

JANE GOODALL

Written by
Alex Woolf

Illustrated by
Isobel Lundie

Franklin Watts®
An Imprint of Scholastic Inc.

Author:
Alex Woolf studied history at Essex University, England. He is the author of many books for children on science topics, including titles in the bestselling *You Wouldn't Want To Live Without* series.

Artist:
Isobel Lundie graduated from Kingston University in 2015 where she studied illustration and animation. She is interested in how colorful and distinctive artwork can transform stories for children.

Editor:
Nick Pierce

Photo credits:
p.27 Ferenc Szelepcsenyi / Shutterstock.com
Shutterstock and Wikimedia Commons.

PAPER FROM
SUSTAINABLE
FORESTS

Published in Great Britain in 2020 by
The Salariya Book Company Ltd
25 Marlborough Place, Brighton BN1 1UB

Library of Congress Cataloging-in-Publication Data

Names: Woolf, Alex, 1964- author. | Lundie, Isobel, illustrator.
Title: Jane Goodall / author: Alex Woolf ; illustrator: Isobel Lundie.
Description: New York : Franklin Watts, an imprint of Scholastic Inc., [2020] | Series: Women in science | "Published in Great Britain in 2019 by Book House, an imprint of The Salariya Book Company Ltd." | Includes index.
Identifiers: LCCN 2019008973| ISBN 9780531235355 (library binding) | ISBN 9780531239520 (pbk.)
Subjects: LCSH: Goodall, Jane, 1934---Juvenile literature. | Women primatologists--England--Biography--Juvenile literature. | Primatologists--England--Biography--Juvenile literature. | Wildlife conservation--Juvenile literature. | Chimpanzees--Behavior--Research--Juvenile literature. | Chimpanzees--Tanzania--Gombe National Park--Juvenile literature.
Classification: LCC QL31.G58 W66 2020 | DDC 590.92 [B] --dc23

Printed and bound in China.
Printed on paper from sustainable sources.
1 2 3 4 5 6 7 8 9 10 R 27 26 25 24 23 22 21 20

CONTENTS PAGE

imPORTANT PLACES IN JANE'S LIFE

ENGLAND

EUROPE

ASIA

AFRICA

Jane Goodall grew up in Bournemouth, England (see pages 6–7).

Jane studied at Cambridge University (see pages 16–17).

Jane studied the chimpanzees at Gombe Stream National Park in Tanzania (see pages 10–27).

Jane accompanied Louis and Mary Leakey on a fossil-hunting expedition in Olduvai Gorge, Tanzania (see pages 8–9).

Jane traveled by boat to Kenya (see pages 8–9).

KENYA

TANZANIA

ATLANTIC OCEAN

INDIAN OCEAN

N
W E
S

INTRODUCTION

Throughout history, there have always been women scientists. But it wasn't until the twentieth century that women like Jane Goodall began to have the professional opportunity to take trips abroad to study the natural world up close and make new scientific discoveries about animals.

Jane Goodall is regarded as the world's leading expert on chimpanzees. Her discoveries revolutionized our understanding of these remarkable animals. Yet she achieved this without any formal training. What she did have was a passion for animals and the patience to study them over long periods in their natural **habitat**. She also had the determination to overcome the **skepticism** of a scientific **community** that did not always approve of her methods.

This book tells Jane's story: her childhood in England, her groundbreaking work in Africa, and her role as a globetrotting **ambassador** of the **conservation** movement.

GROWING UP

Jane Goodall was born in London in 1934. Her father, Mortimer, was a well-known racing driver, and her mother, Margaret, was an author. Jane's sister, Judith, was born four years later. When Jane was one year old, her father gave her a toy chimpanzee called Jubilee. It was named after a real baby chimp who had recently been born in the London Zoo. Jubilee sparked Jane's love of animals, which would last her whole life.

Books She Read

As a child, Jane loved reading the Dr. Dolittle books, about the man who could talk to animals. She also enjoyed the Tarzan novels, which inspired her love of Africa.

I LOVE ANIMALS!

Jubilee

Hiding with Chickens

When she was five, Jane hid for hours in a henhouse because she wanted to see where eggs came from. She had no idea that her family was searching for her.

Dad Goes To War

In 1939, World War II broke out and Jane's father left home to join the army. The following year, Jane went with her family to live with her grandmother and aunts in the seaside town of Bournemouth.

Dreaming of Africa

Jane did well at school, but she couldn't afford to go to college. She worked for a few years as a secretary, but still dreamed about going to Africa and working with animals.

GOING TO AFRICA

In 1956, when Jane was twenty-two, she received an invitation from a former school friend to come and stay on her family's farm in Kenya, East Africa. After saving hard for the fare, Jane took a boat there in April 1957. Seeing Africa and its wildlife was a dream come true for her. She met lots of interesting people, including the famous **anthropologist** Dr. Louis Leakey.

Olduvai Gorge

Dr. Louis Leakey

INTERESTING FOSSIL!

Fossil-Hunting Expedition

Dr. Leakey hired Jane as his secretary. He believed that Jane had the makings of a very good scientist. He invited her to join him and his anthropologist wife Mary Leakey on a **fossil** hunt in Olduvai Gorge, Tanzania.

Jane's Journey To Africa

England
Europe
Asia
Africa
Kenya
INDIAN OCEAN
Tanzania
ATLANTIC OCEAN

Olduvai Gorge, Tanzania

I BELIEVE CHIMPS AND HUMANS SHARE A COMMON ANCESTOR.

Dr. Louis Leakey

Dr. Leakey's discoveries in Olduvai Gorge and elsewhere showed that humans **evolved** in Africa. He was looking for someone to study chimpanzees for clues to the behavior of early humans. He thought Jane might be perfect for the role.

9

THE CHIMPS OF GOMBE

In 1960, Dr. Leakey raised funds so that Jane could study the chimpanzee community in Gombe Stream National Park in Tanzania. As a young woman, Jane wasn't allowed to live there alone, so her mother **accompanied** her for the first few months.

GOMBE NATIONAL PARK

> IT'S NOT LIKE BOURNEMOUTH, DEAR!

Peculiar White Ape

Jane observed the chimps each day. She tried to get them to accept her, but every time she moved closer to them they ran away. Jane was patient though, and gradually they started to accept her. She later said they thought of her as a "peculiar white ape."

WELCOME TO GOMBE NATIONAL PARK

Naming the Chimps

One day, a few weeks after Jane began her study, a chimp with gray whiskers came into her camp. She named him David Greybeard. He was the first chimp who let her come close. Soon she gave all the chimps names to make them easier to identify. Scientists later **criticized** her for this. Usually, **researchers** gave animals unique numbers, not names.

LEARNING ABOUT CHIMP BEHAVIOR

Through patient observation, Jane built up a picture of the way chimps behaved both on their own and as a group. She found that each chimp had its own personality and that they were capable of strong emotions, such as joy or sorrow.

chimps often help each other

Affection and Status

Jane observed behavior such as hugs, kisses, pats on the back, and tickling. She believed these were evidence of affection and **mutual** support. She also noticed that some chimps had a lower or higher **status** than others in the community. They showed this through **grooming**, food-sharing, power struggles, and fighting.

I LOVE YOU TOO!

chimps like to hug to show affection.

HUGGING AND KISSING

A Common Ancestor

Jane was the first person to discover that chimps could exhibit complex personalities and behaviors. She observed chimps using their wits or behaving **deviously** to get what they wanted. This suggested that many behaviors we think of as human may have been inherited from the **common ancestor** we share with the chimps.

PATTING ON THE BACK

GROOMING AND FEEDING

Primate Researchers

Besides Jane, Dr. Leakey recruited two other female **primate** researchers to study the great apes in their natural habitat. Dian Fossey studied gorillas, and Biruté Galdikas researched orangutans.

Biruté Galdikas

POWER STRUGGLES

HE CALLS US THE TRIMATES.

←Dian Fossey

SOME AMAZING DISCOVERIES

Dr. Leakey had helped Jane raise money for her chimp study. She was able to use her time observing the chimpanzees to make several important discoveries about their behavior…

Most people thought chimps were vegetarian

THEY EAT MEAT TOO!

Discovery 1

Hunters

On October 30, 1960, Jane saw David Greybeard sitting in a tree gnawing on the **carcass** of a piglet. This overturned the common belief at this time that chimps ate only fruit and leaves. Jane wondered if he had found the carcass. Later, she witnessed chimps hunting.

Using Tools

A few days later, Jane saw David again, with Goliath. She watched them strip twigs of their leaves, then poke them into a termite mound to "fish" for termites. The chimps were making and using tools! Until then, experts thought that only humans had such skills.

THAT'S SO CLEVER!

chimp with tool

Discovery 3

Chimp Mothers

Jane noticed that female chimps were not born with the knowledge of how to care for their young. They were taught parenting skills by their own mothers. Flo, a good mother, could be **tolerant**, but also imposed discipline when needed. Passion, on the other hand, was a poor mother, who would frequently ignore her children. Flo's daughter Fifi was also a good mother who had many children of her own. Passion's children had few offspring.

Flo's Family Tree

15

THE WORLD REACTS

J ane wrote up her findings and published them in a paper. In April 1962, she gave a presentation to the Zoological Society of London. Many in the audience were not impressed. They didn't think Jane was a proper scientist because she hadn't been to college and had no training. They didn't believe chimps had emotions and personalities, and criticized her for giving them names rather than numbers.

CAMBRIDGE UNIVERSITY

Zoological Society

LET ME TELL YOU ABOUT FLO...

I DON'T BELIEVE HER.

SHE'S JUST A SECRETARY.

SHE'S NO SCIENTIST.

CHIMPS DON'T HAVE FEELINGS.

Going To College

Jane realized that she would only be taken seriously by the scientific community if she had an **academic** qualification. In 1962, Dr. Leakey managed to secure her a place at Newham College, Cambridge, to study for a **PhD** in ethology (animal behavior). She was one of very few people ever to be admitted to study for a PhD at Cambridge University without already having a **degree**.

Dr. Jane Goodall

Jane's supervisor for her PhD was the experienced ethologist, Robert Hinde. He visited her at Gombe and told her he learned more in those two weeks than in all his previous work with animals. Robert, in turn, helped Jane think like a scientist, and showed her new ways of recording **data**. In 1966, Jane was awarded her PhD. She became Dr. Goodall!

PHOTOGRAPHING THE CHIMPS

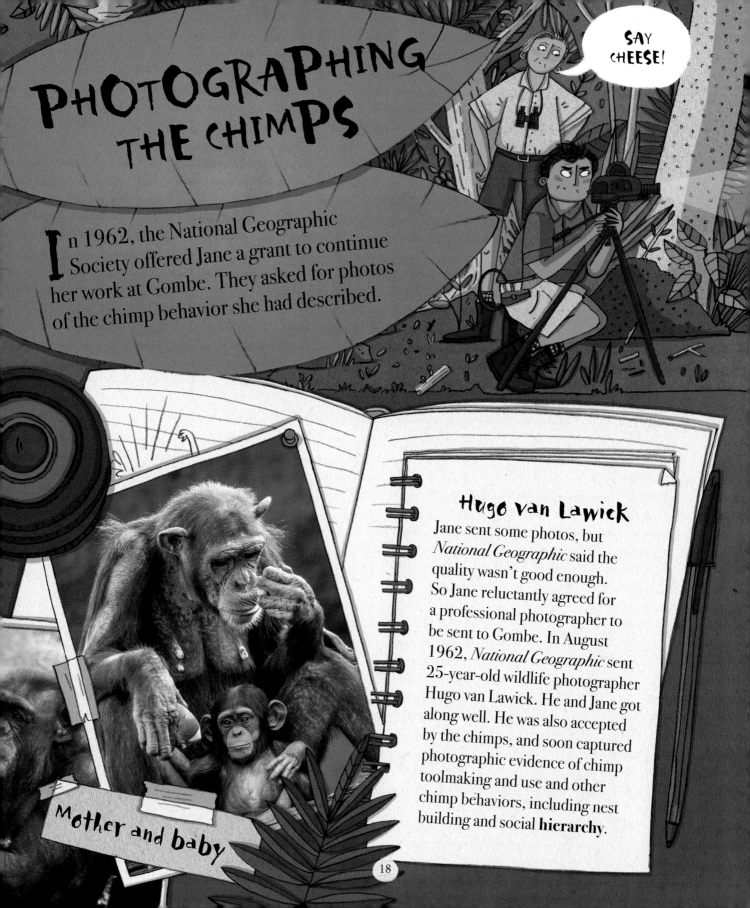

SAY CHEESE!

In 1962, the National Geographic Society offered Jane a grant to continue her work at Gombe. They asked for photos of the chimp behavior she had described.

Hugo van Lawick

Jane sent some photos, but *National Geographic* said the quality wasn't good enough. So Jane reluctantly agreed for a professional photographer to be sent to Gombe. In August 1962, *National Geographic* sent 25-year-old wildlife photographer Hugo van Lawick. He and Jane got along well. He was also accepted by the chimps, and soon captured photographic evidence of chimp toolmaking and use and other chimp behaviors, including nest building and social **hierarchy**.

Mother and baby

A family photo!

In Jane's Words

Jane wrote words to go with Hugo's photos, and *National Geographic* magazine published the story in August 1963.

Jane, Hugo, and "Grub"

Hugo and Jane in Love

During their time working together, Jane and Hugo found that they had much in common. Soon they fell in love. They got married in March 1964, and in 1967 they had a son, Hugo Eric Louis, known to family and friends as "Grub."

FINDING SUCCESS

Jane's *National Geographic* article, "My Life Among Wild Chimpanzees," was a big success. Jane was happy because it raised public awareness of her work, but she wished there had been fewer photos of her in it and more of the chimps. The editors explained to Jane that her story was partly what made the article so interesting.

The Run-Through

In February 1964, *National Geographic* asked Jane to give a major presentation of her work in Washington, D.C. The organizers asked Jane to do a run-through. Reluctantly, she did so, and it wasn't great. She heard them whispering: "Shall we cancel? It's going to be a disaster!"

NATIONAL GEOGRAPHIC

JANE GOODALL

FEB 1964

The Presentation

Once she was in front of the audience, with Hugo's footage playing behind, Jane gave a brilliant talk. She spoke about the need to protect chimps and prevent them from being shot or sold to circuses. She said: "David Greybeard has put his complete trust in man. Shall we fail him?" She pleaded for these amazing creatures to be allowed to live free in their natural habitat.

> WE MUST PROTECT THE CHIMPS!

Jane Makes A Movie

After Jane's successful presentation, *National Geographic* decided to make a film about her called *Miss Goodall and the Wild Chimpanzees*. To make the film, Jane had to reenact a lot of scenes from her early years in Gombe, so Hugo could capture them. The film, featuring commentary by the famous actor and director Orson Welles, came out in 1965. It was viewed by twenty-five million people in North America alone, and brought Jane and her work to worldwide attention.

> MISS GOODALL WENT TO LIVE WITH THE CHIMPANZEES...

Orson Welles

THE GREAT CHIMP WAR

During her time studying the chimps of Gombe, Jane had found them to be similar in many ways to human beings, but thought them "rather nicer" in their behavior. She was forced to change her view in 1974, after witnessing a brutal war break out in the chimp community.

A chimp being aggressive

Derek Bryceson

FRIENDS HAVE BECOME ENEMIES.

I DIDN'T THINK I'D SEE THIS!

North and South

The Gombe chimps broke into two groups: The Kasakela in the north numbered twenty adults, and the Kahama in the south consisted of ten adults. The war lasted four years and ended in victory for the Kasakela, who killed most of the Kahama and took over their territory.

Remarriage

Over the years, Jane and Hugo grew apart. In 1974, they got divorced, but remained good friends. By this time, Grub was living with his grandmother in Bournemouth. In 1975, Jane married Derek Bryceson. As director of Tanzania's national parks, Derek was able to protect Jane's research project. Sadly, Derek died of cancer in 1980.

Shocking

Jane had seen chimps hunting **prey** before, and she knew they could be ruthless. Still, the war shocked and upset her because it was the first time she had witnessed chimps turning on each other, including former friends.

23

CONSERVATION WORK

In 1977, Jane founded the Jane Goodall Institute (JGI) to promote the study and conservation of chimpanzees in the wild. Today, JGI works with local communities to prevent habitat destruction by protecting forests and promoting **sustainable farming** methods.

Goodbye Gombe

In November 1986, at a **conference** in Chicago, Jane was stunned to hear about all the habitat destruction going on across Africa and the threat it posed for wildlife. She knew then that she had to say goodbye to Gombe and dedicate herself to the conservation of wildlife in general.

WE NEED TO PLAN FOR THE FUTURE.

ALL THIS HARD WORK WILL BE WORTH IT!

Lake Tanganyika

DEMOCRATIC REPUBLIC OF THE CONGO

TANZANIA

LAKE TANGANYIKA

ZAMBIA

N W E S

Lake Tanganyika

Roots & Shoots

Jane believed that the best hope for conserving the world's wildlife was to get young people and communities involved, so she launched Roots & Shoots in Tanzania in 1991 and TACARE around Lake Tanganyika in 1994. These programs help people of all ages identify problems affecting humans, animals, and the **environment** in their local community. It then encourages them to develop projects or **campaigns** to try and solve these problems. Today, Roots & Shoots has thousands of groups operating in countries all over the world.

EVERY INDIVIDUAL CAN MAKE A DIFFERENCE!

25

A TIRELESS CAMPAIGNER

Jane Goodall never stops campaigning. She travels an average of three hundred days a year, giving speeches about the threats facing wildlife and urging people to help make the world a better place. She was named UN Messenger of Peace in 2002.

THINK ABOUT THE THINGS YOU BUY AND THE FOOD YOU EAT...

TAKE ACTION NOW!

CHANGE THE WAY YOU LIVE!

JANE GOODALL

Books, Films, and Awards

Jane has written many books, including *In The Shadow of Man* (1971) and *The Chimpanzees of Gombe* (1986). She has been the subject of more than forty films, and she has received international awards for her work. She has come a long way since those days in Bournemouth playing with Jubilee.

WE'LL TRY AND MAKE THINGS BETTER FOR YOU.

chimp of Gombe

Jane giving a speech

Gombe Chimps Today

The chimp community in Gombe, made famous by Jane, continues to flourish. JGI researchers study their diet, health, and behavior. This helps them plan how best to ensure they thrive in the future. Jane visits the chimps every year.

TIMELINE OF JANE'S LIFE

1934
Jane Goodall is born in London, England on April 3.

1960
On July 14, Jane arrives in Gombe Stream National Park to study the chimpanzees.

1957
Jane travels to Kenya and meets Dr. Louis Leakey.

1962
Jane presents her discoveries to the Zoological Society of London.

1940
Jane and her family move to Bournemouth, England.

1960
In October and November, Jane observes chimps eating meat and making and using tools.

1956
Jane is invited by a friend to Kenya. She starts saving up to pay for the trip.

1963
Jane publishes her first article for *National Geographic*, "My Life Among Wild Chimpanzees."

1964

Jane gives a presentation at Constitution Hall, Washington, D.C.

1971

Jane's book, *In The Shadow of Man*, is published.

1991

Jane establishes Roots & Shoots.

1994

Jane launches TACARE, a program to help communities around Lake Tanganyika.

1966

Cambridge University awards Jane a PhD in ethology.

1977

Jane establishes the Jane Goodall Institute.

2002

Jane is named UN Messenger of Peace.

1986

Jane ends her time at Gombe and publishes *The Chimpanzees of Gombe*.

GLOSSARY

Academic
Relating to education and learning.

Accompanied
Went somewhere with someone.

Ambassador
A person who represents or promotes a particular activity or cause.

Anthropologist
A person who studies the evolution and development of human societies.

Campaign
An organized effort, usually involving lots of people, to achieve a goal.

Carcass
The dead body of an animal.

Common ancestor
An animal living in the distant past from which different species, such as chimpanzees and humans, evolved.

Community
A group of interdependent animals living together in natural conditions in a particular habitat.

Conference
A formal meeting of people with a shared interest, usually taking place over several days.

Conservation
The preservation, protection, and restoration of the natural environment and the wildlife that live there.

Criticized
Indicated the faults of someone or something in a disapproving way.

Data
Facts and statistics collected together for study and analysis.

Degree
An academic qualification given by a college or university after an examination or the completion of a course.

Deviously
Do something using underhand methods in order to achieve one's goals.

Environment
The natural world as a whole or in a particular geographical area.

Evolved

When a living thing has developed gradually over many generations. Evolution happens through a process called natural selection: Living things that are better adapted to their environment tend to survive and produce more offspring.

Fossil

The preserved remains of a prehistoric plant or animal embedded in rock.

Grooming

How some animals clean their fur and maintain their appearance.

Habitat

The natural environment of a plant or animal.

Hierarchy

A system in which members of a community are ranked according to their status.

Mutual

Describing an action done by two or more individuals to each other.

PhD

This stands for Doctor of Philosophy. It is a high-status academic qualification awarded to people who have done original research or groundbreaking work in a particular field.

Prey

An animal that is hunted and killed by another animal for food.

Primate

A group of animals that includes monkeys, apes, and humans.

Researcher

Someone who systematically investigates something to establish facts and reach new conclusions.

Skepticism

Having doubts about whether something is true.

Status

An individual's rank or standing within a group or community.

Sustainable farming

A type of farming that conserves the local environment by not using up or destroying natural resources.

Tolerant

Allowing behavior that you don't necessarily agree with.

INDEX